MW01681020

This isn't just a book

It's a love letter to the ones who were broken and brave

To the ones who were never believed

To a horse who trusted again—when he had every reason not to.

A story of scars, softness, and the unspoken language between souls.

A story that will stay with you.

This book is a tribute to the horses that have been saved by compassionate rescuers who provided them with love and trust. It is also dedicated to those who were not fortunate enough to be rescued; Remy's story honors your memory.

With Love,

Shari & Remy

The information presented in this book pertains to the general subject of abuse and is drawn from a variety of sources, including research and public information. No individual's identity or specific case is referenced. Names and identifying details have been purposefully removed to maintain anonymity. The author believes this information serves the public interest by promoting awareness and understanding of this important topic. Some readers may find the subject matter disturbing; please proceed with caution.

Copyright © 2025 by Shari Young

All rights reserved.

No portion of this book may be reproduced in any form without written permission from the publisher or author, except as permitted by U.S. copyright law.

This story revolves around the emotional and physical pain inflicted upon a horse. Horses possess deep emotions, and like humans who have experienced abuse, their hearts, bodies, and minds endure significant trauma.

Allow us to introduce Remy, a beautiful horse with a unique coat featuring auburn red and brown hues, who was born into a world filled with the promise of a wonderful life. Sadly, Remy found himself confronted with challenges he was unprepared to face. The origins of his struggles remain unclear, as he has transitioned through numerous homes.
As they recall his journey, they gain insight into the world as seen through his eyes and felt through his heart.

Faith retrieved a scrapbook from the last cardboard box in their home, her emotions a whirlwind of anxiety, hope, sadness, and excitement. As she flipped through the pages filled with photographs from her youth, and her children's upbringing where memories brought her back: to the simplicity of school in a small town, carefree summers at the beach, the hard work on the family farm during high school, joyful church picnics with friends, and the vibrant rodeo where she first met her husband, JD.

Many young individuals yearn to break free from the confines of small-town life, feeling as though they are destined to repeat their parents' paths. However, Faith was different; she cherished the simplicity and familial bonds that her hometown offered.

Yet, she found herself on the verge of leaving behind her sweet life, uncertain about what the future held. The opportunity presented to JD was simply too enticing to ignore, and after weeks of reflection and prayer, the couple decided to embrace this new chapter, placing their trust in God's guidance for their journey ahead.

JD walked in and saw Faith sitting on the floor, the glistening moisture of a tear apparent on her cheek. “Are you okay, babe?” he asked, wondering if it was too late for second thoughts?

“I’m great! This is hard, but I know God has great things in store for us!” Faith tried to reassure her husband, the crack of her voice betraying her sadness at the thought of leaving her hometown.

JD helped her up from the floor and held her tight. “It will get better. I promise! Now, let’s get these boxes and go pick up the dogs and cat.”

Faith dreaded saying goodbye to her daughter Nicole. She knew she could come visit anytime, and she was never more than a phone call away, but she would never stop feeling that Nicole would need her. She knew deep down that she was the one who needed her daughter. That would never change. Faith's son Riley was in college, and it was another reminder that children grew up and sought out their own adventures. She was also very close to her son, and those goodbye hugs are always hard as well. Mothers never stop worrying about their babies even when they grow up. They can be 80 and still will be your babies.

JD loaded the last few boxes into the pickup truck. Faith got in to drive the pickup and JD clambered up into the cab of the twenty-three-foot moving truck. The truck crammed full of all of their worldly possessions and towed her car behind. She would have to follow him on the drive to their new home. That only made the drive lonelier, but the dogs Tuck and Bella would keep her company.

Faith had an inherent love for animals. They had been a mainstay in her life and mostly all the company she needed. They would make the drive longer, but soon they would have a yard and the freedom to run and play as much as their aging legs would allow.

The two trucks pulled up in front of Nicole's house. The door opened and Tuck and Bella led her daughter out of the house, their tails wagging at the sight of Faith. Faith knelt down and greeted the two dogs, "Hello, babies. Don't you worry. You're going with us this time." Faith looked at Nicole, "Thanks for watching them! It would have been crazy trying to pack with them getting into everything!"

"Mom, don't you think for a minute that I would dream of standing between you and God's plans for you!" Faith's heart ached at the thought of the distance between her and her daughter. Nicole had truly been a blessing in her life, and she would miss her greatly. She knew JD would have her home regularly. "You just remember to visit!"

Faith got up and hugged her daughter tightly whispering, "You know we will!"

JD opened the door to the pickup and helped the dogs into the lifted Chevy, getting them situated in the back seat. Faith looked at JD.

"I think we're really doing this," Faith said, her voice soft.

"We are," JD replied. "And we'll make it home to visit."

Faith and Nicole said goodbye one more time, a hug that lasted half of an eternity.

As JD climbed into the moving truck and Faith adjusted her seatbelt in the pickup, she looked into the rearview mirror one last time. Nicole stood at the end of the driveway; her hand raised in a steady wave. Faith held her breath, willing herself not to cry again.

The sight of her daughter growing smaller in the mirror felt like something final, even if it wasn't. With a deep breath, she whispered, “Okay, God. I'm trusting you.”

The drive stretched out ahead—miles of highway bordered by rolling hills, thick woods, and the occasional small-town diner with signs that hadn't been updated in years. The kind Faith would have loved to stop at. She had packed sandwiches and snacks, but there was comfort in the idea of sliding into a vinyl booth, ordering a slice of pie, and listening to someone else's story.

Tuck and Bella shifted in the back seat along with the cat, Ry. They were old now, but loyal to the end, resting their gray-muzzled heads on the seatbacks and looking forward with tired curiosity.

The hours ticked by slowly. Even though she thought JD drove too slowly, the moving truck was always just a few car lengths ahead, his steady hand on the wheel like a beacon for Faith. She prayed along the way—small, simple prayers. Prayers for safe travel, for strength, for peace. For courage to face the unknown.

They stopped at a rest area just before dusk. JD stretched his arms above his head as he walked over to Faith. "Still doing, okay?"

"I think so," she replied. "Though Bella's snoring may be a hazard."

They laughed together, letting a bit of the tension melt. They sat on a bench for a while, eating the sandwiches she had packed. There was beauty in that simple meal—no distractions, no noise, just the two of them and the soft hum of insects in the grass around them.

“Do you ever worry we’re chasing something that’s not even there?” Faith asked, her eyes trained on the horizon.

JD was quiet for a moment. “All the time,” he admitted. “But I’d rather take the chance with you than wonder for the rest of my life if we missed something we were meant for.” JD leaned in and said “maybe you will have a purpose in this move, God might be using you for something. “ Faith laughed and said “You might be right” But then she thought of what might lie ahead—a new church to serve in, neighbors to meet, maybe even new friends to welcome into their life. JD's new position was more than just a job. It was a calling. And she believed in that calling.

Faith was excited at the thought of living in a house near the beach. Excitement took over as they reached the last hour of their journey. The truck in front of her slowed and her phone rang with a familiar tune, she knew it was JD.

"We have a problem…" JD grumbled. "This truck isn't going to make it; I have to stop."

Faith found herself questioning whether this move was God's will as JD pulled the moving truck off the main highway to the gated entrance of a small farm. JD got out of the moving truck and threw his hat on the ground, frustrated that they had come so far.

Getting out of the truck, Faith asked, "What's the matter?"

“The truck is overheating! If I drive it further, it might have to be towed. I’ll call the roadside assistance number. But there’s no tellin’ how long we will have to wait for a repair.” JD looked angry. JD was a good man, but he was a rugged and tough cowboy that expected things to work.

Faith stepped closer and laid a hand on JD’s arm. “It’s okay. We’ll figure it out,” she said gently. He nodded but didn’t speak, his jaw clenched in frustration.

They stood in silence for a moment, the sun dipping lower in the sky, casting long shadows across the gravel turnout. Behind them, the land stretched out—wide and open, with pastures rolling gently under the golden light. In another circumstance, it would’ve felt peaceful. But now, it just felt like another bump in a long, uncertain road. Faith was so surprised such beautiful countryside was so close to the beach.

JD pulled out his phone and called the roadside service. Faith walked back to her truck, opened the door, and let the dogs out. Tuck and Bella stretched and sniffed around, seemingly unbothered by the detour. She envied them for their ability to adapt without worry.

As the dogs wandered, she looked back at JD. His broad shoulders were tense as he spoke on the phone. It wasn't just the truck. She could see it. The stress of uprooting their lives, the pressure of starting something new, the weight of being the one who had pulled them away from all they'd ever known—it was all catching up to him.

She called the dogs back and walked toward him, slipping her hand into his free one. He glanced at her, the furrow in his brow softening slightly.

“They’ll send someone out within the hour,” he said. “I’m sorry, Faith. I should’ve had this checked before we left.”

Faith shook her head. “Don’t do that. It’s just a delay. Not a sign. Not a failure. Just a delay.” Trying to convince both JD and herself.

They sat on the edge of a nearby fence while they waited, the dogs laying at their feet. A soft wind moved through the grass. Faith looked up at two large figures moving toward them. “Is that horses?” she queried.

Two horses approached the gate, curious to know who was coming to visit them. Faith hopped down from the fence, “Oh, be quiet!” She chided Bella for barking at the horses.

Faith cautiously approached the first horse, reaching out to pet him on the nose.

The horse leaned forward, ears twitching as Faith's hand reached for its muzzle. Its velvety nose was warm, and its breath tickled her fingers. There was something grounding in the moment -something that made the chaos of the last seven hours pause.

"Well, hello there," Faith whispered, smiling softly. The second horse moved closer, nudging her side. "Aren't y'all friendly?" she said, glancing over her shoulder at JD.

He had turned toward her, watching her interaction with the horses with a half-smile tugging at the corner of his mouth. "Looks like you're already making friends."

Faith chuckled. "Maybe they're here to remind us, we're not the only ones adjusting to something new."

JD rose from the fence and joined her at the gate, petting the other horse. "I didn't know how much I needed to see you smile right now," he said, resting his other hand on the wooden slats beside her.

She leaned her head briefly on his shoulder. "I didn't either."

A pickup approached the gate from the farm. Momentary concern dashed through JD's mind, hoping they had not offended anyone. The truck stopped as it approached the gate and a sweet woman emerged. "Hi folks, everything alright?" Faith responded as she continued to caress the horse, "Everything's perfect."

"Well," JD interjected, "our moving van broke down. We're waiting for roadside assistance. I hope we're not causing you any trouble."

"Not at all, I was just wondering what stirred their curiosity. My name is Amy, I see you have already met Tuff and Nika." Amy pointed to the light black horse Faith was petting, “Nika seems to like you.”

“Hi Amy, I’m JD and this is my wife, Faith.”

“Is this your farm?” Faith asked.

“This is Horse Haven Retirement Farm, it’s a safe place for horses in need, whether they come from kill pens, abusive situations, neglect, or even from caring owners who had to find them new homes. I have a few volunteers, who help out, and Elizabeth, who helps me with daily operations.” Amy explained. A few years ago, Amy founded the Horse Haven Retirement Farm and made her dream a reality by opening this nonprofit organization.

“And who is that?” Faith asked, pointing at another horse standing about fifty yards away. The horse had a beautifully distinctive coat with auburn red and brown hues.

“Well, that, my dear, is Remy! Poor guy has had a rough life. That’s about as close as he will get. He hasn’t gotten within twenty feet of a person since he’s been here!” Amy clarified.

Faith remembered her time working the farm down the road of her childhood home and Taboo, the ornery horse who had trusted only her. Faith felt a sense of God’s purpose growing inside of her. Faith abruptly turned to Amy and asked, “What can I do?” Amy raised an eyebrow, slightly taken aback by Faith’s sudden, heartfelt question. She looked into Faith’s eyes and recognized something she hadn’t seen in a long time—genuine compassion, not just for animals, but for the brokenness they carried.

“Well,” Amy said slowly, carefully choosing her words, “we could always use an extra pair of hands. Especially hands like yours.”

JD looked over at Faith, who was now completely absorbed in watching Remy. His frame was strong, his spirit clearly weary. There was a silent hurt in the way he kept his distance, yet an unmistakable pull in how he hadn't completely turned away. Faith nodded, her voice quiet but certain. "I want to help. I don't know what your schedule looks like, or if you're even taking volunteers, but... I've got time. I'm good with horses, and I know what it's like to be scared and not know who to trust." Amy smiled, the kind of smile that comes from watching God work through unexpected moments. "You've got yourself a place here anytime, Faith. We always say, the horses find their people. Maybe Remy just found his."

Faith's heart swelled with something she hadn't expected to feel so soon after leaving home—a sense of belonging.

Just then, the sound of a diesel engine rumbled in the distance. JD looked down the road and saw the roadside assistance truck approaching. "Looks like help's here," he said, touching Faith's arm. "We should get ready."

As the mechanic pulled up beside the overheated moving van, Amy touched Faith lightly on the shoulder. "If you're serious, come by any time after you get settled. The farm is always open—especially for hearts like yours."

"I will," Faith promised, meaning it with every fiber of her being.

Faith continued to talk with Amy as the moving truck was fixed, planning to come back.

"Let's go!" JD exclaimed.

As they pulled into their new neighborhood, the darkness had already settled in, enveloping the surroundings in a serene quiet.

Their new home stood proudly, adorned with white shutters that exuded a charming, coastal ambiance. The porch light illuminated the front steps with a welcoming warmth, inviting them to step inside.

Faith parked the pickup truck and swung open the back door, allowing their dogs to leap out. Tuck and Bella cautiously explored the unfamiliar yard, their tails wagging with excitement despite their aging bodies. Ry the sweet cat meowing to say I am still here too.

JD emerged from the truck and joined Faith on the porch, where they shared a moment of stillness, absorbing the significance of their arrival.

“We made it,” Faith murmured, her voice quivering with a mix of joy and nostalgia.

Throughout the night, her thoughts were consumed by the farm, her anticipation bubbling over as she envisioned the work that awaited her there.

Even as they settled into their new routine over the next few days, her mind kept drifting back to the horses, particularly Remy, whose presence tugged at her heartstrings.

One evening, JD decided to fire up the grill, and as they sat outside, basking in the breathtaking sunset that painted their backyard in hues of orange and pink,

Faith turned to him with a spark of enthusiasm. “JD let’s call Amy at the farm. I really want to go up this weekend and see what help she needs.” JD nodded in agreement, recognizing that this visit could be just what Faith needed to fill the void apparent in her eyes.

With excitement bubbling within her, Faith reached out to Amy to ask if they could visit the following day, and Amy's enthusiastic response only fueled her eagerness. The rest of the evening was spent in animated conversation, filled with dreams of meeting the horses that Amy had mentioned, some of which they could see grazing in the distance, their silhouettes framed against the fading light.

The following morning, Faith rose with the sun, her excitement overflowing as she anticipated the day ahead. JD, an early riser by nature, was already in the kitchen when she emerged, and he couldn't help but ask, "Faith, why are you up so early?"

With a bright smile, she replied, "It's horse day, and its's time to get started." Her inability to contain her excitement was unmatched, even on their wedding day.

As they prepared to head to the farm, JD took the dogs out for their morning walk while Faith dressed in her well-worn jeans, a faded shirt, and her trusty cowboy boots, ready to embrace the adventures that awaited them.

Faith's enthusiasm was infectious, evident to anyone who saw her. She rummaged through the refrigerator, gathering apples and carrots to share with the horses, and after giving the dogs a treat and a warm hug, she made her way to the truck. JD started the engine, and as Faith hopped in, her face lighting up with a beaming smile. The two of them drove along, the music playing softly in the background, while Faith chatted about her eagerness to meet the horses, her words flowing like the excitement bubbling within her.

As they arrived at the farm, the familiar sight of the gate adorned with the farm's logo greeted them. Faith took out her cell phone, dialing Amy to gain access. After a brief moment, Amy's cheerful voice came through the line, assuring her, "I'll open the gate now." With that, Faith and JD drove through the entrance and onto the long, gravel driveway. As they made their way down, the vibrant sounds of the farm could be heard, they spotted chickens pecking at the ground and a proud rooster strutting about. Glancing toward the expansive fields, Faith's eyes lit up at the sight of horses grazing peacefully, donkeys nearby, and the most adorable goats frolicking in the grass, adding to the charm of the idyllic setting.

Amy, JD, and Faith sat together, their conversation flowing effortlessly as Amy painted a vivid picture of the farm. It was a stunning place, not just for its lush green pastures and the sturdy buildings that provided shelter for the animals, but also for the symphony of sounds that filled the air. Among these sounds was the pounding of hooves, particularly from a striking horse named Roy. A former racehorse, Roy showcased his remarkable speed and elegance, his mane blowing in the breeze as he ran captivating everyone with his beauty.

Unlike the typical stalls one might envision, the horses here enjoyed the freedom of outdoor enclosures, allowing them to roam freely rather than being confined to a barn. You could tell these horses were loved beyond belief and a little spoiled.

As Amy delved deeper into the stories of the horses, Faith listened intently, particularly drawn to those who had been rescued from dire situations, such as kill pens or abusive environments. When Amy spoke about Remy, a horse who remained distant from humans due to his traumatic past, Faith hung on every word, her heart aching for the gentle creature who had yet to learn to trust again.

As Amy spoke, Faith found herself captivated by the thought of Remy, her mind momentarily drifting as she absorbed Amy's words. With a sense of urgency and purpose, Faith interjected, asking, "Amy, could I make Remy my mission? I want to work with him because I can't bear the thought of him leaving this world without feeling love and trust again." Amy's response was filled with heartfelt appreciation as she replied, "Absolutely, Faith. All the horses here are aging, and we can't predict how much time we have left with them. It would truly be a blessing for you to work with Remy." A radiant smile spread across Faith's face as she eagerly inquired, "When can I start?" Without hesitation, Amy replied, "Right now," and together they made their way to the field, ready to embark on a journey of connection and healing.

As they walked through the field, Amy, JD, and Faith were warmly introduced to the charming residents of the farm: a lively group of horses, gentle donkeys, and a handful of spirited goats. The goats, brimming with enthusiasm, eagerly approached the trio, clearly thrilled to meet new friends. The donkeys, with their calm demeanor and lovable charm, nudged and nuzzled the visitors.

JD and Faith had come prepared, bringing along a stash of treats that quickly became the highlight of the day, as they discovered that all the animals shared a common love for snacks. Amidst the laughter and playful chaos, Faith turned to Amy with a grin, suggesting that it might be wise to distribute the treats closer to the barn, as the goats seemed to be taking charge of the treat distribution, playfully competing for attention. Their shared amusement echoed through the field, creating a joyful atmosphere that celebrated the delightful connection between humans and animals. However, one donkey decided to vocally start his braying which echoed loudly through the field. He was a handsome donkey with a beautiful spirit. JD, Amy, and Faith all laughed over how loud he was.

After interacting with all the animals, the group gradually made their way toward Remy, who stood observing them with a calm demeanor. They maintained a respectable distance, allowing him the space he needed while still ensuring he could hear their cheerful greetings. Faith, in particular, was captivated by Remy; she locked eyes with him and attempted to engage in conversation. However, as they drew nearer, Remy chose to retreat, leaving Faith with a sense of disappointment. She felt a bit sad, believing that this moment was a missed opportunity for connection. Yet, her resolve only strengthened; she was determined to find a way to work with him, convinced that with patience and understanding, she could bridge the gap between them.

Faith could not help but think that if horses could speak, what would they reveal within the depths of their emotions. Faith knows horses possess an innate ability to recognize those who hold significance in their lives.

Faith prayed in that moment God would help her get through to Remy, not knowing she was about to experience a profound connection unlike anything she has felt before.

Every day Faith would visit the farm, accompanied by JD as his schedule allowed. JD would complete fence repair and work on the barn while Faith was intentional about distributing treats to all of the animals. She would brush out the other horses and leave an apple on the fence post for Remy. For the first few days, Tuff or Roy would beat him to it as Remy carefully watched on. Faith would cautiously hold her hand up and take a step toward Remy and Remy would respond by shaking his head and turning to walk away. Each visit would culminate with Faith inquiring more about Remy, curious about his background. Amy shared a captivating tale: in a serene countryside, a mare settled on the rolling hills to give birth, and on that day, a remarkable colt emerged, eager to explore the world. With dreams and ambitions, he was determined to fulfill his potential. While the exact origin of his name, Remy, is uncertain, it is thought to stem from the Latin "Remigius," signifying remedy and healing. Faith felt a deep connection to this name, as Remy's story embodies themes of recovery and renewal. Even as Faith fell deeper into Remy's story, she would not yet see the vital role Remy would play in her own healing journey.

As Amy continued, she said “we know some history; from a young age, he was put to work as a cart horse and spent many years in that role.” Faith and Amy knew while pulling a cart may be seen as labor for a horse, it doesn't have to be strenuous when done correctly, with an appropriate load with appropriate age. Starting a horse too young can cause future implications depending on the horse's breed and training. Horses, especially those bred for such tasks as draft horses, can pull impressive weights on wheels with ease. For a well-cared-for horse, pulling a cart can be as manageable as a person pushing a fully loaded shopping cart.

“I’ve heard that breeds like Clydesdales and Belgians are specifically designed for heavy hauling,” Faith shared, “but it's essential that they receive regular breaks and proper nutrition to maintain performance and their health.”

Amy replied, “Problems arise when horses are overworked or when smaller breeds are tasked with pulling loads that are too heavy. They’re easily injured and can have long recoveries..”

Faith said, “Is it true that many of these horses end up sold to auctions, slaughter or other owners when they can no longer work?”

Amy replied, “Yes, they can also suffer from mistreatment after being pushed to their limits. However, the majestic Clydesdales we all admire in commercials, are lovingly cared for and cherished by the right owner. Horses begin their journey of training to pull carts at the tender age of two, a time when they are still growing and not yet ready to bear the weight of a rider, as their joints are still maturing. While guiding a cart along smooth terrain is less taxing than carrying a rider, it's important to remember that pulling heavy loads can still take a toll on their young bodies. If a young horse shows signs of struggle or if an older companion is starting to slow down, it's a gentle reminder to pause and honor their needs."

Faith asked; "It's sad, I don't know how anyone can hurt these beautiful animals."

Amy stated "Remy's past as a cart horse remains a mystery, leaving us to wonder about the issues he faced.

Starting his journey at such a young age and eventually being sold, it's likely he bears some hidden scars."

Faith quickly replied, "I'm so glad he made his way to you Amy! You are giving him an amazing life. "

As Amy continued her story about Remy's past, Faith listened attentively learning about the hardships that undoubtedly affect Remy's spirit. There were so many gaps in Remy's story, a fact that strengthened Faith's resolve to connect with this amazing animal. Amy said "His past remains a mystery with many untold stories and countless homes. When fate dealt him a cruel hand, leaving him unable to work due to injury or other hardships, he was sold away like a forgotten treasure."

Faith with her heart hurting said "The number of homes he may have known after that is lost to time then."

Amy said, "What we do know is that he eventually arrived at a farm, where he encountered further hardships, a heart yearning for kindness amidst the shadows."

Faith replied, "this is so sad how he had to bear this in his life, especially when things took a turn for the worse."

Amy continued to share that one of those homes was where his struggles continued. He endured that abusive environment for many years, almost a decade we were told.

Faith went home that evening wondering, if Remy had the chance to share his experiences, would he express his deep resentment towards his owner(s), his longing for freedom, and his belief that he didn't deserve the mistreatment? Did he ever contemplate escaping?

The next morning found Faith with a fever and sinus infection. The pollen had found her. More hurting from the disappointment of not going to the farm, she was sentenced to bed by JD, who always did a good job of nursing her back to health. She sent Amy a text, telling her she would be out of order for a few days, and decided she would call Nicole. “Hi, mom!” Nicole answered, “How’s the unpacking?”

“Nicole you wouldn’t believe!” Faith’s voice betraying her illness and her excitement over Remy. “Mom, you sound terrible!” came the reply.

Faith began to relate the experience with the farm and the mystery of Remy. “I can’t believe I am not out there today. I just know I am getting through to him!”

“You will, Mom, just get some rest. Love you!” The concern evident in Nicole’s voice as she said goodbye.

Faith spent the next two days wondering if Remy would see her absence as abandonment. Would she have to start all over in building his trust? Remy’s background was filled with sorrow, and those who mistreated him only contributed to a spirit of uncertainty and mistrust. Horses are magnificent creatures, they are still animals, much larger than us, and they have the capacity to inflict harm. People have a greater capacity to inflict pain or torment on a horse. As with many animals, this fosters fear, anxiety, and lasting behavioral issues. Faith desperately did not want to be the reason for any of his fears.

Her fever broke after two days, and she ignored JD’s pleas to rest for another day.

Faith enthusiastically drove to the farm and started her routine giving treats to the goats, donkeys, and the horses. As she stroked Roy's muzzle, she felt a gentle nudge. She turned slowly to see Remy behind her tugging on the bag of apples in her hand.

Amy watched in bewilderment as a smile beamed across Faith's face and tears of disbelief streamed down her cheeks. Faith choked back an audible sob and simultaneous laughter, trying not to startle Remy. She slowly reached into her bag and pulled out the largest apple she could find. Remy hungrily accepted the gift and slowly backed away. He looked at Faith, "*I want to trust you*," was the message delivered, and a deeper connection made, all with a glance. The loving attention Faith had given to all the animals had paid dividends, and now the door was open.

Momentarily shaken by the connection, Faith wondered whether she should share the experience or wait to see if there was more to the message. She called JD immediately. “JD, the most amazing thing just happened! He walked up to me! He ate an apple right from my hand! He told me that he wanted to trust me!” Her excitement carrying her right through the whole encounter.

“Wait, who said what?” JD responded, obviously puzzled.

“I don’t know how to explain it. He walked up and nudged me and tugged at my bag of treats. I fed him an apple, but then when he walked away…” she hesitated.

“What happened?” JD wondered if Faith still wasn’t feeling the effects of the sinus infection.

“Well, he turned and when he looked at me, I just got this overwhelming feeling that he wants to trust me! I could feel his heart! I just know I am getting through to him.”

“It sounds like it! Just don’t forget to be patient with him!” JD warned, knowing his bride’s propensity to break the sound barrier whenever she gets excited about something! “I’ll see you at home, tonight! Love you!”

“Love you too, JD,” Faith responded, not convinced JD believed her. She finished out the day, brushing out Roy and Tuff, looking over at Remy, just to see if he was watching her.

The sun was setting over the tree line and Remy was again keeping his distance. Amy and Faith concluded that the earlier encounter was all they could hope for on this day, although the days to come would prove Remy’s eagerness to share the story of his life. Remy would begin to reveal the experiences that shaped him, sharing the challenges he has faced and the triumphs he has celebrated.

A week passed before Remy approached Faith again. She treated him to a carrot and dared to caress his cheek. Remy brushed his nose on Faith's arm and looked up at her. Again, she felt a connection with Remy. As Faith sat with Remy, she let him take the lead in their conversation, encouraging him to share his story from the depths of his heart.

"I've always envisioned a life filled with love, delicious meals, and a bit of indulgence. Instead, I found myself in a harsh environment governed by strict rules and severe consequences for even the smallest errors."

Faith told him "You're safe now! No one can hurt you here. Amy, Elizabeth, and I will take good care of you!" Faith responded with a tone of reassurance as she slowly picked up a brush and seeking Remy's approval to brush his coat.

As she brushed his coat, Faith continued in disbelief as Remy shared his journey of resilience and hope, filled with moments that have tested his spirit and defined his character. She gained insight into his dreams, struggles, and the unwavering faith that has guided him through the ups and downs of life. This wasn't just a story; it was an invitation to understand the depth of his experiences and the lessons he learned along the way.

Faith says to Remy "*It's bewildering for me; I feel you didn't deserve this fate. The reasons behind the decision to inflict pain on you remain a mystery. Are you suffering from the toll of years spent pulling a cart, making even simple tasks painful? Did you endure hunger and confinement when you couldn't meet expectations? So many questions linger, yet the motives for the cruelty are lost to me.*

Remy replied "In that place, my spirit began to fade; I endured beatings for reasons that were beyond my comprehension. I recall the times I was struck with a piece of wood, leaving behind scars that would never fully fade.

Tears were streaming down Faith's cheek as Remy's experiences were revealed to her.

"Are you okay?" Amy asked.

Faith took a second to gather herself. "This poor animal! There is no justification for such brutality!" I wish I knew how to use his experience and highlight the silent suffering of all horses who endure similar fates.

Remy continued, "*Despite the pain and mental torment, I clung to hope, wishing for a way out. Days turned into years, and only I knew the true extent of my daily struggles. I tried to hide from the torment while doing what was necessary to avoid punishment, but gradually, I felt my heart and will to live fading away. Where was the compassion? Would anyone ever come to my aid? Each day brought fresh pain, and I awoke dreading what lay ahead."*

Faith looked at Amy. "Remy has been through so much. It's no wonder he is so fearful…so distrustful."

Amy explained, "Horses are naturally prey animals, and can show aggression when they sense danger. Many traumatized animals may exhibit aggression as a means of self-protection, stemming from their broken trust and deep-seated fears. This behavior often arises not from a desire to harm, but rather as a defensive response to perceived threats in their environment. Understanding this can help us approach these animals with compassion, recognizing that their actions are rooted in a need for safety and security. We must understand what triggers their fear responses - things like unexpected loud sounds, unfamiliar surroundings, or the presence of other animals can be really scary and stressful. Having a harsh owner who doesn't treat them with kindness and respect can exacerbate their anxiety and fear, putting them even more on edge."

Faith looked back at Remy, "Can you tell me something good?"

Remy began to tell Faith about the unwavering companionship of a magnificent horse named Paint, his best friend. "*Together, we faced the harsh realities of our environment, our bond growing stronger with each passing day. It was clear that Paint, too, felt the weight of our struggles. Just imagine the fear that gripped our souls, yet we clung to one another, our connection so profound that separation felt unbearable. As the years slipped by, anxiety loomed over me and Paint, each day a reminder of the potential for more suffering. But fate had a different plan in store, but we did not know it because we did not know anything but harshness.*

"One overcast day, while we were grazing in the field, a woman named Alice arrived, her presence a beacon of change. She approached with purpose, ready to take Paint away. I watched in confusion and dread as Alice began to harness my beloved friend. Panic surged through Paint as he glanced back at me and I was overwhelmed with emotion, if I could have, I would have tears streaming down my face as I paced in distress. Alice paused, her heart aching at the sight of our impending

separation. As she loaded Paint into the trailer, Paint gazed back at me, his eyes filled with sorrow, while my cries echoed in the air. In that moment, Alice felt compelled to act. With compassion in her heart, she turned to the owner and, seeing the despair in my eyes and hearing my screams, asked if she could take me too. To her surprise, the owner shrugged, showing his disdain for me, and said, "Take him." And so, in that moment of kindness, a new chapter began for both me and Paint, united again in the embrace of love."

"Alice was an angel saving me. I was so upset and scared that it took them a while to catch me, but Paint kept telling me it was okay to come with him. I didn't want Paint to leave by himself, so I finally calmed down and got to join my buddy and settled down in the trailer for our new journey. Unfortunately, I was still

scared of humans and emotionally scarred but Alice was unable to get close to me, she still loved me and took care of me. I was grateful to be leaving behind a place I could never truly call home, as a real home is filled with love, not cruelty. While I felt some relief, I was still uncertain—was I being taken to an auction, a kill pen, or yet another abusive owner? If only I could have known I was finally going to be safe. Healing isn't easy for us just like humans, trust and love is hard to regain."

A wave of relief passed over Faith as she had finally felt something positive. She looked over at Amy and asked bluntly, "What ever happened to Paint?"

Amy was shocked and bewildered as she had totally forgotten about Paint, and she was certain she had never mentioned him! "How...how do you know about Paint?"

Faith, realizing that Amy was surprised of this connection with Remy, wasn't sure she didn't look a bit crazy at the moment. "Remy told me?" she answered with hesitation.

Amy stared further in disbelief, but she could not deny what she knew to be true. "Paint and Remy were rescued from an abusive owner. They were virtually inseparable. Paint may be the only reason Remy survived. Did you know that horses are capable of cognitive memory and can recall past experiences, which means they can develop behaviors similar to PTSD in humans after experiencing trauma. With his background, Remy most likely had a touch of this. Remy was frequently yelled at or mistreated."

Remy continued "*I remember those negative experiences and I became fearful and cautious. Additionally, I felt the pain just like humans do when we are whipped, as our nervous systems allow us to sense discomfort. Hitting us leads to both immediate pain and long-lasting psychological issues. As you all are starting to understand, I have some issues. It's important to note that our skin is sensitive like human skin, we feel the pain. It's important to remember that there's never a justification for mistreating me and other horses. While we can't express our feelings in words, those who know us well can often tell when something is wrong.*"

Faith was starting to understand that she could read Remy like no one else.

Remy could see that Faith was not like a new horse owner, and she was familiar with basic care and maintenance. "*Most of us love regular grooming and it is not only necessary but also a fantastic opportunity to strengthen your bond with us. We all love a little pampering. We also require consistent healthcare, including hoof trimming, which some of us are not too fond of. It's important we receive treatment for any illnesses or injuries.   We need safe shelter, and companionship is crucial as well. Additionally, take the time to learn about different breeds and our temperaments, some of us have more temperaments than others. Owning us is a significant financial responsibility, we are sorry about that, but we appreciate you and we demand daily attention. Finding the right horse for you and offering them love, patience, and care is key. Don't let any other horse have to go through what I did. It truly breaks our spirit."*

Paint and I have finally found ourselves in a nurturing haven, where the gentle hands of sweet Alice showered us with love and care. As the years unfolded, life blossomed beautifully for us, but I still have my insecurities and am not sure how to fix them myself.

However, as Alice's health began to fail, she faced the heart-wrenching challenge of continuing her devoted care for us. With a heavy heart, she made the wise decision to seek out someone who could assist her in looking after me and Paint. Her deepest wish was for us to find a loving new home, where we would be cherished just as she had cherished us. I do regret that I would have been not so afraid, but I am trying to heal, I just can't do it alone. I think it is going to take a special person to help guide me. Although Alice was kind, things take time, and I just could not open up yet."

"Me and my best friend, Paint, were loaded onto a trailer, ready for our new adventure. Alice felt a wave of sadness wash over her as she watched us leave, but she also had faith

and hope that we would be all right. As the trailer rolled down the driveway, she waved goodbye, tears glistening in her eyes. Her bond with us ran deep; even though I often struggled to accept human affection, she sensed that I held a special place for her in my heart. She was the first person to truly reach me, who had made a lasting impact on my life. She did save us both from beatings. I guess you can say we were touched by an angel for the first time."

"I'll bet you could have stayed with Alice forever." Faith whispered to Remy. Amy looked on with continued disbelief. It was getting late, but Faith's curiosity was overwhelming.

Amy chimed in, "There are many heartfelt reasons why caring owners might have to say goodbye to their horses, whether it be due to financial struggles, health concerns, or other life circumstances. These animals possess remarkable memories, particularly those in the wild, who create deep connections with their herds. The act of separating any of them can be incredibly challenging and may impact on their demeanor and spirit. This is where compassionate new owners and rescuers come into play; with love, patience, and understanding, they can find comfort in a new environment and among new companions, but it seems they still miss their old friends. If they ever unite with an old friend again, they will remember them. It typically is a breathtaking reunion for all to watch. They are social beings, flourishing in groups, as the togetherness offers protection from threats. The thought of being alone can be quite frightening for them. Anyone needing to rehome a horse needs to invest time in finding a loving and appropriate new home. Taking the time to research potential options and seeking recommendations can ensure they transition to a deserving and caring situation."

As nervous as Remy was he said "*Alice dedicated herself to finding a wonderful man named Colby, who generously offered to take us in. He was a cool guy and seemed to know a lot about us. A true rescuer at heart, he vowed to help us discover our new homes filled with love. Under Colby's gentle care, I began to blossom, as Alice opened my heart to the possibility of a brighter future. With each passing day, I started to embrace the kindness of Colby. Paint and I thrived in our new sanctuary, surrounded by lush pastures and the companionship of other horses. This is where I met Sugar and Roy too. We all shared several joyful years together until the tragedy struck when my friend Paint, my best friend, got sick and was taken away. The loss shattered me; I roamed the fields searching for my beloved companion. Colby would tell people and described it as one of the most heartbreaking scenes he had ever witnessed. I didn't know what happened to Paint. I wish I could have said goodbye, but I am told that experts suggest that allowing the surviving horse to see the body of their departed friend can aid in understanding the finality of loss, helping us to grieve. It's essential, however, to let us approach this moment at our own pace. I do believe this would have helped but sometimes we know it's not possible, but all I know is that I miss my friend and always will."*

Headlights suddenly came around the corner, spooking Remy who trotted away. JD hopped out of the truck. "Was that....???" He asked in disbelief.

Faith, a bit upset, answered "Yes, that was Remy! He was opening up to me." Faith continued excitedly, telling JD about how Remy told her the stories of Paint and Alice. JD's expression betrayed the extent of his doubt.

Amy chimed in, "I know it sounds incredible JD, but there are some things Faith could not possibly know about Remy!"

"Okay, well let's go home, you probably shouldn't be out in the night air. You'll get fever again!" JD replied, a slight tone of condescension in his voice.

"Okay, okay!" Faith said begrudgingly before shouting "Good night, Remy!"

Faith shared more of Remy's story with JD on the ride home. His hangry grunts of disbelief aggravating her at every turn. She knew JD was having a hard time believing her, but the fact that he saw Remy next to her was undeniable. She said a prayer of thanksgiving before bed, grateful that Remy had started to bond with her, and hopeful that the relationship would build.

The next morning, JD accompanied Faith to the farm to help with some repairs. Amy had taken great care of everything, but there is always something to build or repair at the farm. He walked toward the house as Faith gave the requisite treats to the goats and other horses.

He watched in amazement as Remy walked up to Faith and brushed his nose against her. "What is it, boy? Did you have a good night? Faith asked.

Remy ate his apple and as Faith reached for his face to pet him he shook his head, indicating no, but he did not walk away. Faith slowly picked up the brush again to listen to more of Remy's story "*I started forming a bond with Colby, yet I kept others at a distance, I still didn't trust anyone, and it got a little worse with losing Paint. My heart ached from the loss of my best friend. During this time, I met Roy, he was cool and used to be a former racehorse who began to reach out to me in my grief. Slowly, I started to rediscover moments of joy with my friends. Colby, who cared deeply for me, took time to reassure me. As we were aging, he decided to retire me.*

My friend Roy had a limp; he still possessed a grace that made his limp disappear when he ran. He was a stunning and gentle soul, and as our friendship blossomed, Roy became a source of comfort for me. Colby made the heartfelt decision to retire Roy, Sugar, and me together."

Faith was saddened that Remy had to move again. He had found friends in Paint and even Colby but moving was traumatic.

"*This decision led to us being transported to Horse Haven Retirement Farm, a place where love awaited us but again, we were scared. Once again, I found myself in a trailer, but I had Roy and Sugar with me. Coming from a nurturing home, we felt reassured about our destination, knowing Colby would never send us to a harsh place. Upon our arrival at the farm, we were greeted by Amy, the warm-hearted owner of Horse Haven, who welcomed us with open arms and overflowing affection. As we were unloaded, Roy eagerly embraced the love of our new home, basking in hugs and kisses, while I, still a bit hesitant to accept the kindness surrounding me. Sugar was a sweet girl, and she loved Amy immediately. I looked around and there were several more horses, donkeys and some goats, this place was pretty cool."*

"I heard Colby and Amy talking that in 2022, Amy, the founder of Horse Haven Retirement Farm, made her dream a reality by opening this nonprofit organization and how much she loved horses. That was a great sign and so good to hear. They spoke about how the farm serves as a safe place for horses in need, whether they come from kill pens, abusive situations, neglect, or even from caring owners who had to find them new homes. This is where I fell in love."

Amy is a kind-hearted and selfless woman who has dedicated her life to caring for horses. She has a beautiful spirit and has created a home where we feel loved and cherished. We have found the perfect place to retire, one that exceeds our wildest dreams. This farm is a safe haven for sure because one of Amy's most remarkable ideas for the farm is that we all are never adopted; we stay here for life, until we run free in heaven. We receive regular veterinary care, food, grooming, and, most importantly, love and trust. You all know me now; I still don't get any of these fun things because I still fear humans, but I do like the food and treats. It is amazing to me that Amy runs this farm financially herself most of the time, but the farm relies on donations to support us and any future horses that need a loving retirement home. We tell any new horses that arrive how cool it is and although some of us might be little distance to the new guy and gal, they all warm up eventually, but for me I become their friend and show them around. I do better with horses than I do with humans."

Amy and JD walked toward Faith. Remy, still cautious of JD, started pulling away from

Faith. JD immediately backed off and gave Remy space.

“Amy, where is Sugar?” Faith asked.

Amy shot a glance at JD. “Um, Sugar passed about six months after she arrived with Remy and Roy. She is buried over by that tree, but how do you know about her?” Amy asked, knowing the answer.

“Remy told me! I know you think I am crazy, but he is telling me his whole life story.” Faith insisted, turning her attention back to Remy. “I’m fixing lunch, so come to the house in a few.” Amy declared.

“I’ll be right in…” Faith responded. She could hear Amy telling JD that she had never told Faith about Paint or Sugar. She laughed to herself and started brushing out Remy once again.

Remy explained "*I could sense that Amy adored all the horses, and all of us shared that love, but I could see you were particularly determined to help me rediscover love and trust. I hear you expressing your desire for me to experience those feelings before ever leaving this world, making it your mission to help me open my heart again.*" *Every weekend, you dedicated time to all the horses but always made sure to spend extra moments with me. I'm sorry I was so damaged it was hard for me to open up. You brought me treats, chatted with me, walked alongside me, and persistently tried to get closer. You understood that this journey would require immense patience. Even though I just had no trust in anyone anymore, you were very sweet to me."*

Faith found tears streaming down her cheeks again. No one had ever recognized her acts of love and kindness.

"*Every weekend, you followed the same routine, but one day something changed. When you raised your hand, I didn't back away; instead, I shook my head from side to side, indicating I wasn't ready. You understood and reassured me it was okay. I was beginning to trust you, as I chose to stay close instead of running away. I even surprised myself. Days turned into weeks, yet you remained steadfast in your efforts with me."*

JD shouted from the house for Faith to come to lunch. Reluctantly, she told Remy to go play with Roy and she would be back after lunch. Faith walked toward the house. Remy followed for a few feet, "I'll be right back!" she said, causing Remy to stop.

When she arrived at the house, Amy and JD could see the evidence of the tears Faith had shed. “Now, what has you all conflicted? JD asked.

“Nothing! I just love that horse!” Faith replied, not wanting to feed JD’s doubts with further explanation.

“I have to go to town after lunch to get some lumber for fence repair. Do you want to join me?” JD asked.

Amy looked on, knowing what the answer would be, hoping it would not cause a fight. “No, I have to tend to the horses” Faith fibbed, knowing she just wanted to be with Remy.

The three finished lunch and JD headed off. Faith looked at Amy, “He thinks I’m crazy, you know?”

“I think he’s starting to believe. I know I am. I told him about how you knew about Paint and

Sugar. Now, unless you went out and found Colby, I'm not sure how else you would know any of that!?" proclaimed Amy.

"I know Remy thinks you're amazing! He's so grateful to be here!" Faith added, getting up from the table, a knowing smile stretched across her face. Faith and Amy walked back outside toward the horses and began tending to Tuff and Roy.

Remy patiently waited for Faith to finish with Roy and walked up to her. "I guess we're not done with you today are we, Remy?" Faith asked. He shook his head, and she began to brush him.

As Remy continues telling his story "*As many of us have had tough lives, it is important to foster trust with horses, it's important to grasp our behavior and engage in brief, consistent sessions. You consistently employ positive reinforcement and establish boundaries, while also honoring my limits until I feel comfortable. You don't give up easily.*"

"*We all appreciate having clear guidelines, but once we retire, we tend to enjoy a more relaxed lifestyle. You always seem attentive to my body language, which helps you understand my feelings. You're very in tune with what makes me anxious or nervous, and always respond with patience, opting for shorter, routine sessions. I am starting to love this girl.*"

JD arrived back at the farm and started unloading lumber. He pulled a 2x4 out of the truck and Remy bolted with fear. Remy looked

back and saw how Faith had reacted. Calm and full of compassion, Remy sensed her concern for him.

"In that moment, Faith recognized the panic in my eyes and worried that they had set me back. However, she spoke gently to me and at that moment I knew she was going to do anything to protect me. I eventually returned, knowing that while I was scared, I could be comforted.

The routine continued, and as the weeks passed, she kept striving to reach my heart. She would talk to me and pondered what more she could do to earn my trust, determined that one day I would come around. That day arrived sooner than expected. How can I say no to this angel? She showed me love that was so incredible, she refused to give up on me."

After calming Remy, Faith met Amy and Elizabeth at the house. "Amy, you are right Remy is losing weight. I know I see him eating, but his energy levels seem to be dropping too. Did you say the vet should come look at him?" Amy replied, "Yes I am going to get him checked out."

"JD and I have to go back to Georgia for a few days. Riley is graduating, and we are excited to watch him walk." Faith was thrilled at the prospect of seeing her son again and eagerly anticipated that warm, heartfelt hug. Faith was very close to Riley and so proud of him.

"Go say goodbye to your boy. We will take good care of him, and if anything changes, we will call you!" Amy replied.

Faith feigned a smile and walked out to Remy, caressing his shoulder and softly explaining how she would be gone for a few days. "I wish I could take you with me, but Amy will take good care of you as always." Remy nodded. He knew he did not feel right, but he decided that he would hold onto Faith, and thoughts of her while she was gone. Remy watched as Faith rode off with JD.

Remy reminisced "*I remember it was a beautiful sunny day, with a few volunteers and Amy present, Faith offered me a treat and gently reached out to pet me.*

To everyone's amazement watching I allowed her to stroke my side, they all started crying, tears of joy since my stubborn fear seemed to be releasing. They captured the moment on video, so I was the star now.

Faith got in the truck waving to me with so much happiness so I can only imagine she left that day with a heart full of happiness, eagerly counting down the days until she could see me again. I think she loves me.

Each time Faith and I reached new progress and they all recognized that while they could now pet me, there was still much more to do. I was still in the mindset; ok, petting is okay but not sure about all that other stuff. She began experimenting with different approaches; she could touch my side but not my face. My face was one of the places I used to get hit on and that still brought fear to me. Faith knew introducing a harness and lead would take time for me. Eventually, Faith and Amy decided to let me into the pen area, as it was challenging to catch me in the open field, especially with the other horses acting as my protectors. We all cover each other's back. I just knew going into the pen area I would get some oats, and more treats and Faith was pretty nice, so I was truly starting to trust her.

During our time in the pen, I continued to enjoy treats and feed while Faith gradually approached me. She introduced me to the purple lead rope, a color she adored, likely influenced by her love for LSU, as she often wore their shirts. Her passion for football was evident, and it made sense that I ended up with the purple lead. It was soft to the touch, she allowed me to sniff it before gently placing it around my neck and then taking it off. I had them on before, but one person beat me with that too, so it was fearful. I can tell you I will never like this person or anyone that beats us. This was a positive step for the day, considering I had deep emotional scars, fearing that humans might harm me. For the next few days, Faith continued using this same gentle approach. One day, she took the lead rope and lightly wrapped it around my neck, walking me around the pen.

She said I did remarkably well, and we shared a sort of conversation; she spoke to me. Did I tell you this girl can talk? I responded with soft sounds, but I was telling her I loved her, but

humans don't know our sounds, but they know our hearts, she probably knew. I remained calm and relaxed as we walked together. Faith felt a connection growing between us and she was right; I felt it also. The next goal was to get a harness on me. After a few more walks around the field and some heartfelt chats, she decided to try the harness. To everyone's surprise, even mine, I simply accepted it, I said, "Go ahead." Now, she could successfully use the harness and attach the lead, marking a significant achievement in our journey together. I was starting to be proud of myself, who was this girl and how did God know I needed her? I love it.

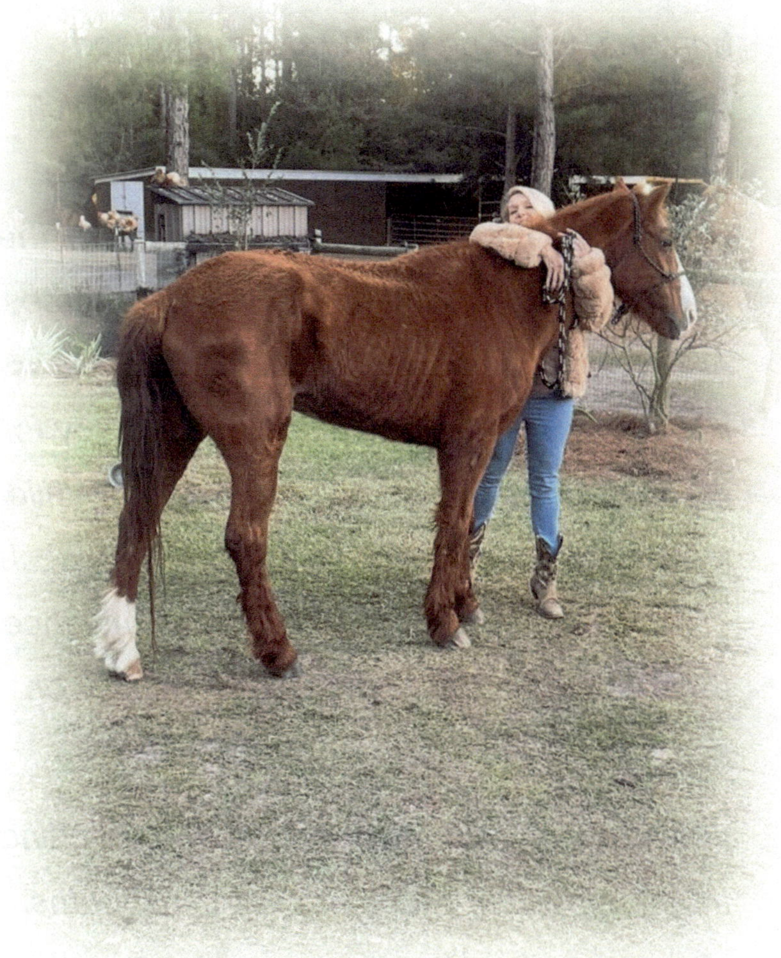

Faith and I were enjoying each other's company, and in my presence, she found a sense of peace that made her worries fade

away. It felt as if time had paused in a serene moment. We have a unique ability to soothe humans, lowering heart rates and blood pressure while boosting endorphins, which helps alleviate stress and anxiety. We are remarkable creatures who can also calm the human nervous system. Additionally, horses are sensitive to human emotions and intentions, making us valuable in therapy for those dealing with stress and trauma. While Faith may not possess all these qualities, she certainly experienced the soothing influence that I and the other horses at Horse Haven can offer.

I love being around my friends and watching them enjoy their grooming sessions, baths, and pampering like human pedicures. However, I prefer to keep my distance for now, as I'm not quite ready for that level of indulgence! Faith, on the other hand, is determined to help me join in on the fun. Some horses really relish their grooming time, and it makes her a bit sad that I haven't experienced it yet. So, yes, you're right—this is her next mission with me. I saw this coming! After several weeks of walking, talking, and getting me used to the harness and lead, she decided to start with just brushing to see how I would respond. Oh, and I forgot to mention that she can give me hugs, which I absolutely adore! As she began brushing me, I relaxed and enjoyed the gentle massage. Seriously, who would not enjoy a massage, now I know what I was missing out on! The next step was introducing shampoo to me. At first, I was a little unsure, but I handled it well. She was trying so hard, I had to work with her, and it felt good to have a clean coat. Pretty refreshing. I was starting to like this pampered life.

Not me anymore, but many horses can be frightened by the hose, but if people approach us gently and pay attention to our body language, ears, and eyes, you can tell when we are calm or anxious. If we pull our ears back tight, we might need reassurance. If we are pawing at the ground it is something we do naturally, but it can also mean a few different things. *We might be trying to uncover food, especially if we're hungry. Sometimes, we are just exploring interesting things. It can also show that we're feeling uncomfortable for various reasons, or it might reflect our emotional state, like boredom or frustration. Roy is a good one for pawing telling you he is done with the bath, and we all laugh. Although it's not very common, it could even be a sign of colic. So, it's important to watch us closely and take the right steps to help us out. If we start to get nervous, it's best to take it slow, allowing us to acclimate gradually. With time, we learn to trust and adapt.*

Faith and I have developed a strong bond, who did not see that coming? Even though I am not quite there with everyone, I trust Faith completely and seek her care. I even started to return her hugs and lean into her when she embraced me. She is just so caring, who can resist.

Crop

After a few days, Amy walked out and saw that Remy was on the ground. She tried to get him up, to no avail. She knew she had two calls to make, first to Faith and then to the vet.

The morning after graduation, JD and Faith were out to breakfast with Riley and Nicole, their first family meal in months. The conversation drifted from discussion of Riley's future to Faith's exciting narrative of her connection with Remy. Faith's phone rang, and JD noticed her smile fade away to an expression of concern, when she saw that it was Amy.

"Amy, is everything alright?" Faith begged.

"Well, he's on the ground and not able to get up. I'll have the vet here in the morning, but I was thinking you might be able to help get him up?!" Amy explained.

"Put me on FaceTime!" Faith asked.

Amy complied and held the phone near Remy. Remy responded, "*Amy reached out to Faith via FaceTime to see if she could provide some motivation. I'm not sure if it was the sight of her face, or the compassion in her voice, but I knew I had to try to get up, for her. This was the first time we ever used FaceTime to support me, but after Faith encouraged me, I managed to get back on my feet. That was a sweet gesture.*"

JD, Riley, and Nicole watched in amazement at the impact Faith had on Remy.

After the call, Faith looked at JD, "Can we go back tonight rather than in the morning?" I want to be there for the vet in the morning. Remy will be so scared."

Nicole did not wait for JD to say no. "Of course you're going back tonight, Mom!" she stated, giving a look of defiance to JD, daring him to refuse.

“We’ll go get checked out of the hotel and head back early tonight!” JD says with a tone of disappointment. JD and Faith enjoyed the company of family and would’ve spent three more days following the kids around, but even JD felt this was a priority.

Faith spent the entire drive in silent prayer, thanking God that Remy was able to get up and asking that she make it back to him before it was too late.

The next morning Faith and JD arrived at the farm just before the vet. Remy held onto Faith. I have lost weight, so Amy decided to call the vet to get me checked out. While the vet examined me and took some blood Faith held me, comforting me and letting me know everything was fine. I would lean my head against her chest for some extra comfort, showing how much, I trusted her. The vet mentioned that many years ago, when I was younger I might have broken my hip at some point and hadn't received proper care, but thankfully, it doesn't bother me now and I walk normally. They felt relieved to hear that, but I know Faith and Amy were sad to think about how someone had ignored my pain in the past. Faith told me we are now just waiting a couple of days to figure out how to help me gain weight back. They feed me a lot with great stuff. I was doing so well, but I lost it faster than they hoped. The next morning, Amy calls Faith because I fell again, and I am having trouble getting up. Faith and her husband JD showed up to the farm and came running over to me. I was struggling to rise. The vet gave them some advice, and they made sure I kept eating, which I did, love my food.

Remy looks at Faith, "*I want to get up, but I don't have the strength*." A tear runs down Faith's cheek.

As time goes on, their concern grows since I am still down, and I am concerned too. They pull the trucks into the field for better light and decide it is best to be with me. Who does this, spends the night with me in the middle of a field to make sure I am okay.? Faith, JD, and Amy are pretty special people, but it did make me feel better along with my other horse friends.

The night is chilly so they cover me with blankets to keep

me warm. They roll me over to help with blood circulation and massage my legs. That helped and made me feel better.

I know I am in trouble, but I call out to my other friends, who come over, showing me, I am not alone, and Roy was one of the first to run over. The night drags on, and they stay up checking on me, warming up in the truck when they need to. I doze on and off, and they play music and talk to keep me company. Faith played some cool music. I liked her choices.

As the 24-hour mark passed and I was still down, their worry turned into tears. I dislike seeing Faith so upset, I know how much she loves me, and I love her too and I want to get better. Faith spent the entire next day by my side, not leaving me for a moment. She didn't know what would happen, but she wanted me to feel her presence. At that moment, JD, Faith, Amy, and Elizabeth gather around. They figured I might see humans differently from the four of them around me.

Faith played music and talked to me, expressing how much she needed me and that she didn't want me to leave them just yet, but it was my choice to fight. *"I don't want to leave either I will fight until I can't anymore, I love this place and all of you."*

It was heartbreaking for them to see me fighting to stand up. I put in so much effort all day, pushing myself up and even resting my head down to gather strength, but every time I looked at Faith, it was clear I desperately wanted to rise. Unfortunately, my back legs just wouldn't cooperate, leaving me frustrated. Each day, my caregivers would offer me comfort, but they also had to roll me over frequently to prevent the sores forming on my legs from my relentless attempts to get up. I could hear them calling the vet again, fully aware of what they would say since it was now day three of me being down. Their hope was being tested, but their faith remained strong. I felt sad for them and me. They decided to return to the barn, while Faith and her husband said they planned to go home for some rest, Amy who promised to call them if anything changed. Faith gave me such a big hug with tears falling on me, but her heart hurt her too. Before they left, Faith insisted they had to roll me again to help improve circulation in my other back leg if I had any chance of getting up.

Elizabeth, along with Amy, JD, and Faith decided to take a chance and roll me because they were running out of time. They needed to get my knees bent so they could turn me over. After massaging my legs, wondering what was happening, I relaxed and started cooperating, but that didn't last long. As they were rolling me, I kind of freaked out and suddenly tried to get up. We all found some adrenaline we didn't know we had, and they managed to keep me steady until I gently settled back down, allowing them to roll me over.

I was comfortable eating, and Faith took a moment to be with me again. While she was talking to me, I lifted my head and looked directly into her eyes, I was really listening to everything she said. Elizabeth watched in awe at the connection between us.

Before she left for the night, Faith looked at Remy and whispered, “If you want to run free, God is good, and even though I would miss you a lot and love you dearly, it’s ultimately your choice.”

She also expressed how much I had helped her, teaching her about love and trust, rather than the other way around. She will never know how much I grew with her, and my heart was hers.

I love her name because her name, Faith, truly reflects her character as she possesses a deep sense of inner belief. She took the time to encourage me to reach out to God for assistance, fully aware that I might not understand what she was suggesting. Maybe I do and maybe I don’t, but it soothed my heart. Despite this, she decided to give me the opportunity to explore this path, but she realized that I required additional support to find my footing.

No one can really know what goes on in any horses' mind or heart, but I knew and was ready to fight, and a lot of people were praying for me.

I watched as Faith said she was headed home, but I could not help but sense she was feeling heartbroken.

Amy checked on me every two hours, she is an incredible soul who always takes care of all of us. I heard Amy tell Faith she would provide updates on me and with calls and texts to Faith.

I can only imagine that each time, the news was the same, and so was Faith's mood.

Amy was talking to Elizabeth, and I overheard that Faith took to Facebook, posting about a "Sunday Miracle" and asking for prayers for me, sharing a beautiful Christian song that pleaded with God to lift me up. I know how utterly defeated we all were feeling. Amy said Faith decided to get some sleep around 3 a.m.. But at 4:30 a.m., she heard her phone beep and jumped up to see a text that said, "He is the same." She went back to sleep feeling hopeless, knowing that the longer I stayed down, the more dangerous it became for me.

I was trying so hard and wanted to get up and finally I did. I wanted to call Faith myself, but horses don't have phones. This thought even made me laugh.

Amy came running out and started videoing me again. Making me a star again.

Amy called Faith just after 7 a.m. "He is up"

Faith screamed in the background "Oh God, you both did it! He's up!" Without wasting any time, Faith and JD were pulling into the driveway. Faith jumped out of the truck and ran straight to the field. I was munching on the grass and hanging out with the other horses. I looked at her and was excited to see her but needed some more strength and food, so I looked at her, "*Give me a minute; I'm just loosening up my legs.*"

About an hour later, I came over to the barn area to be with Faith and the others, allowing her to pet and hug me. “*Thank you*.”

This was definitely a miracle, and they believe that both God and I played a big part in it. No matter what you believe, this God seems to be something that makes Faith happy so it's all good; today they witnessed something amazing, a true miracle, and we're really grateful.

OFFENDS YOU
GOOD LAUGH

After the initial thrill of seeing me get up, I ended up lying down again for another two days. With rain and colder temperatures on the way, Faith and JD came to the farm.

After two hours of trying to lift me with Amy, I just couldn't budge. So, the three of them had to think outside the box; they rolled me onto a heavy-duty tarp, secured it with a bracket, and attached it to the truck to pull me to the stall. Faith oversaw, keeping me calm on the tarp, a challenge she was ready to take on. Roy ,Nika, River and Tuff and the other horses gathered nearby, their curious eyes fixed on Amy, Faith, and JD, silently questioning what they were up to with me.

Suddenly, all the horses burst into a spirited gallop, a breathtaking sight as they danced across the field. They were also wishing I would get up to join them. They approached me and Faith, Amy, and JD again, and if the humans could hear them, they warned one another, "Don’t lie down; they might haul you away with a truck!" The horses all laughed, yes, we can laugh inside. Beneath their playful antics, there was a shared concern for me, as they too sensed the unease in the air, wondering if they had lost their minds.

To everyone’s surprise even the other horses were following, they managed to get me in front of the stall, at a slow and steady pace. They all exchanged glances, realizing they would need to roll me into the stall next. They came up with another plan to get me a bit closer, with Faith and Amy encouraging me to stand and walk a few steps into the stall. As they tried to inch me closer, I felt I could try and help, surprisingly I got up! Everyone was thrilled as they led me into the stall, finally able to breathe a sigh of relief.

The situation was confusing as they still didn't understand why I was lying down and unable to get up.

Just after getting into the stall, Amy's phone rang. It was the vet. The blood test results came back, revealing that I had cushings, which they all suspected but worse they found out I also had EPM, which stands for Equine Protozoal Myeloencephalitis. This is a neurological condition in horses caused by protozoan parasites like Sarcocystis neurona and Neospora hughesi. Essentially, these parasites come from possum droppings and can be found in hay and fields, which horses might ingest while grazing. They learned that I had a severe case and had likely been suffering from it for many years, even before my previous owners and not showing symptoms. The vet also told them that this is not contagious to other horses and humans.

Everyone anticipated the next recommendation, especially given the seriousness of my condition and I had it for years prior to arriving at Horse Haven.

I watched as Amy and Faith discussed the situation. "I know you don't believe me, but he still has fight left in him, I can feel it!' Faith proclaimed.

Amy questioned the advanced stages of my condition. Maybe one day they can find a test that can detect it earlier, the older we get and the more advanced, it can be hard to manage. They were right, I didn't want to leave them either, I love it here and love them too. Although they were prepared to hear that I might need to be euthanized, they also didn't want me to suffer without a decent quality of life. This isn't the conversation anyone wants to overhear, but I know they were going to fight for me. After several discussions about my future, Faith, who had never heard of EPM before, decided to research it. Unfortunately, the more she looked, the bleaker the information seemed. However, she stumbled upon a post about Potato Patch Farms, which mentioned horses that had been cured using a special nutritional regimen with natural blended products for EPM. This was sounding promising.

Excited, she called the woman from the farm and then brought Amy into the conversation. After speaking with Peggy at Potato Patch Farms, their hope began to rise. Peggy was incredibly knowledgeable and seemed like a true blessing. Peggy was still concerned about my age and how far advanced my condition was. She provided guidance on what steps for Amy and Faith to take and instantly sent a two-week supply of the products, ensuring that they wouldn’t have any delays in starting my treatment.

Faith prayed they had found the answer and Amy began giving me these natural products, they were pretty good too and the best part is that they are safe for me and packed with vitamins. They can even cross the brain barrier to eliminate the parasites that can cause serious issues. After just 24 hours, I was lying down and getting up on my own. To everyone's surprise and happiness, I was responding well to the products.

The next day, I managed to break the stall lock with a little help from my equine buddies, and I surprised Amy in the morning. She was shocked and said, "Oh no, you need to rest!" so she replaced the lock. She put me back in the stall and my buddies were laughing, how rude!!!

I am a social horse who loves being around my pals, so I was not too happy about being cooped up in the stall. However, I enjoyed taking walks with Amy or Faith. As time goes on, I started to venture out on my own, but

Faith or Amy would catch me and tell me time to go back to stall and sometimes I would return on my own because I knew I could sneak some peanut hay and feed without my buddies trying to steal my meals. Some of us get a little food aggressive.

I have recently embarked on my recovery journey, and everyone remains hopeful and optimistic as they observe my decreasing struggles. I am feeling better and doing good. Amy faced a difficult decision regarding me; despite my physical challenges, I exhibited a strong will to fight. I believe because Faith really pushed me. Faith shares a profound connection with me, as if she understands that I know she will advocate on my behalf and explore these products. The options were to either let me go, okay that is a depressing thought or to take a chance, knowing that they had nothing to lose—either the treatment would be effective, or it would not. They chose to do the treatment. Regardless, they would never allow me to suffer, as they would recognize when I was ready to give up. Thus far, they are thrilled to see my positive reactions and the resurgence of my strength, and so am I.

Faith and Amy are aware that I am getting older. I am 26 years old, and my age is becoming more apparent. Like any of us getting older, we feel and sometimes see the weathering. They cherish every moment with all of us, especially since their beloved Tuff is already 39 years old. He is the old guy at the farm, and we all respect him, so he runs us off sometimes. He is slowing down too but he looks out after us all.

Tuff

It has been months now and I am doing better. With the love from Amy, Elizabeth, JD, and Faith's dedication to my health; they find comfort in knowing that if the time comes for me to leave them, I will be running free in Heaven with love and trust in my heart. My time with them has been filled with trust and affection, and their healing efforts have truly made a difference in my life. I have learned to love life rather than to dread it. Here's to them having many more wonderful years with me, and they eagerly anticipate each day filled with those warm hugs. They have given me so much love and more time, although I am sick, I keep on keeping on.

My story isn't just about how I conquered my fear of humans; it's also about raising awareness of the mistreatment of horses and all animals. While they may not know every detail of my life, I do, and they do know I suffered abuse and needed to heal. Despite my past, I have a heart and mind that I was once frightened and hurt. It is still scary to think of how cruel people can be. Thankfully, through love, patience, and care, I have learned to trust and love again. I still can't believe Faith and how hard she loves me. I hope my journey will inspire others to speak up for horses who have been silenced. We all ask for your kindness as we share the same capacity for emotion that you do. Our hearts may be larger, covered in fur, but our spirits are uniquely vibrant and deserve a good life.

The day came when another horse arrived. Amy had rescued a horse from a kill pen who was defeated, emaciated, starved, and lacked muscle. When he stepped off the truck, everyone felt a wave of despair, unsure if he would survive. I joined Roy, Tuff, and my other friends, we all stood around and thought about this poor horse and what was his story? I heard Amy say that vets were worried too, but then I saw Faith spend a night with him in the stall, encouraging him to pray and telling him that if he wanted to live, he needed to try to walk. I was a little jealous, Faith was my savior. Faith came over to me to say good night then headed home. Amy also named him Clint, cool name.

This was the weirdest story I heard so far, but the next morning, Faith arrived at the farm, and Amy jokingly asked if she wanted to pray on her lottery ticket. First, I never heard of a lottery ticket, but it must have been something good.

Looking at Faith's face, you could tell she was confused, but Amy revealed that Clint had walked across the entire field that morning. I was thinking to myself, yes, we all watched that, what is the big deal? I get it now, we all watched Clint grow bigger and I used to go into the pen with him, we loved it for the extra feed and treats. Clint is a strong and handsome horse and it's amazing to think that all it took was some prayers, love, Amy's, and Elizabeth's daily care, and plenty of food since he was so malnourished.

Today, he's a happy and sweet horse and solid mass. Here it is me losing weight, but I am getting there, but Clint is a big horse now. Everyone is always amazed by his transformation. This farm is not just a sanctuary for horses; it truly helps heal our minds and hearts.

Let's give a shout-out to all the horses, me included, that need the support, the caring rescuers that step up to help them, and the forever homes that offer endless love. Hope and pray you all find an Amy, Faith, Elizabeth, and JD team!

It's important to treat animals kindly because both physical and emotional abuse can cause lasting harm. Look at me, it was a rough life at times until I got here. We don't deserve any of that. We're so grateful for the amazing rescue and forever home organizations that provide love and trust, giving all animals a chance to have a happy life. Right now, I am facing my own struggles, but they can tell I know they are here for me. I have finally found love and trust, and hope I get to enjoy many more years of this, it's truly amazing. I just wish they found me earlier in life. But they also understand that one day I will run into heaven, but you can bet I am taking their love with me. My heart is so full.

Many people are invested in my story, and they all believe that Faith and Amy are like angels for me. I must agree they are pretty special.

Faith managed to help me overcome my fear of being touched by a person. She trusted her intuition; it is the primary channel through which we can connect with you on a spiritual level, feeling an inner sense of knowing. That is how Faith found Potato Patch Farms, that gut feeling that a possible cure is out there. Her determination is unwavering; she refuses to back down, and thankfully, she persisted in healing me.

As a result, I now get to experience so many wonderful things, like those incredible massages that I had previously overlooked due to fear. I learned not all humans are bad, the cure was love!

They may not be certain how my age will influence my healing journey, but what they do know is that I am getting up, and they are pouring all their love and effort into supporting me.

I have to admit, it is the best feeling ever! Ultimately, Faith has fulfilled her mission to ensure that I feel love and trust in my heart, never allowing me to leave this world one day lonely and scared. She is truly awesome, and I love her back. I often think about my dear friend Paint, whom I lost, and I believe that when we meet again, he will be proud of the horse I've become, fearless now!! Faith and Amy are so proud of me. The absence of Paint weighs heavily on my heart, and lately, Faith has been sharing memories of him, which helps me connect with the love we shared. I think it is Faith's way that has made me feel love again.

Roy has come up in our conversation before, and here he is again, checking in on me like a loyal friend. He's doing well and spends a lot of time with me, and together we cherish our dream home. Love is truly the most beautiful aspect of life; it has the remarkable ability to heal. I've been learning this lesson from Faith, and I'm finding joy in life, especially in the sweet hugs, kisses, and treats she shares. She really is the coolest.

I might have good and bad days, but Faith and Amy always make it a good day. So far it is all good days.

Roy & Remy

I heard Amy calling Faith one morning to let her know that I was down again. I can see Faith and JD to driving fast down the farm driveway, the gravel was kicking up from the tires and I could see her blonde hair flowing from out the window and looking at me in the field. I could see Faith jump out of that jacked up truck, barely hitting the ground and running towards me. She seemed to be in a state of panic; she held me in her arms as I was struggling to rise. I was showing her my determination to get back on my feet, it just was so hard for me to get up.

Faith recognized my fighting spirit and clung to the hope for a miracle, praying fervently to God in front of me and everyone, though I could feel she felt uncertain about why her prayers seemed unanswered, trusting that it was all part of a greater plan. My horse buddies gathered around, sensing the effort to help me, and Faith and Amy provided me with water and food that I loved.

You can truly say, they spoiled me, and they would make fantastic nurses, they both have caring souls. Just like before, they had to keep rolling me to prevent stiffness, and this continued for a couple of days. As night fell, the hope for my recovery rested heavily on everyone's heart, including my own. Faith spent hours in the field with me, petting and talking to me. She had such a gentle touch that went through my soul and relaxed my fear. Her constant expressions of gratitude and affection made each minute feel like an eternity. Despite my efforts, I recognized how fortunate I was to have her by my side; her presence lifted my spirits and brought me comfort.

I would attempt to rise, sparking excitement among everyone, only to fall back down, prompting a rush to catch me. I felt an overwhelming sense of frustration, yearning to heal and reunite with the people who had profoundly impacted my life. I really loved Faith, Amy, Elizabeth, and JD, I don't want to leave them. My thoughts often drifted to Paint, perhaps because the uncertainty of my own future weighed heavily on me. Horses can be scared and fearful.

I could see the pain that both Faith and Amy were facing with me. Amy understood the difficult truths Faith was avoiding, questioning when it would be fair to consider my quality of life. Faith saw a spark of determination in my eyes and kept hoping for just one more day, convinced I would stand again.

I must confess that my heart lit up in Faith's presence; she was the beacon of hope I desperately needed, restoring my life without a hint of fear. Faith understood me in a way no one else ever had, intuitively grasping my thoughts and feelings, and she was always attuned to my every action.

While Amy shared that hope, it was painful for both of them to witness me unable to get up, knowing that horses shouldn't remain on the ground for too long due to safety concerns. Despite the challenges, Faith clung to her belief in my fight, supported by Amy, who stayed by my side day and night. Faith kept telling me that when she gets home that her and JD will pray for me to be up by morning, but as they pulled into the farm the next morning, they see that I am still down bringing them disappointing news.

As another day passed, I found myself lying down when Amy decided to reach out to Faith, informing her of my struggles. During their FaceTime call, Faith's words were filled with warmth and encouragement; she was almost pleading, and I could sense the urgency in her voice. Her heartfelt support brought a glimmer of hope amidst my challenges. She was truly my best friend now.

Suddenly, I could hear Faith say she noticed a figure above the barn area in the blue sky where I was lying, prompting her to ask Amy about it. Amy insisted there was nothing there, but Faith was convinced it resembled Jesus. She believed the image signified either a coming for me or a healing. Faith and Amy sent the picture back and forth, trying to decipher it, realizing some things might be beyond explanation.

Faith mentioned on the call she would be heading to the farm soon, and I felt a surge of excitement, even while lying on the ground.

Faith looked at JD. “How am I going to get through this? I’m not sure how I can say goodbye to him! He was cheated out of so much, and just when he is learning to trust again, he loses the strength to fight!” “Baby,” JD responded, “ before you came along with Amy, Remy would have died lonely. He knows you love him, and even if that was just for a day, it is still love."

Faith knew she couldn't abandon Remy, no matter how hard it got. She had given him permission to go before, and perhaps she would have to again.

The couple arrived at the farm again, and Faith cradled Remy's head in her arms again and asked in a whisper, "Is it time, boy? It's okay if it's time."

I understand how challenging this situation is for all of us. As animals, we often have a deeper awareness of death than humans do.

Although I was reluctant to let go, my body was simply failing me. Thankfully, with Faith by my side, my heart remained strong and healthy.

When Faith arrived at the farm, she immediately sensed a shift within me; my eyes conveyed a deep love, as if silently signaling that my time had come. In that instant, the memory washed over her, and she realized that whether it was merely a fleeting thought or a divine message, God was urging her to accept the difficult truth: she would have to let me go.

As tears welled in Faith's eyes, she took a moment away from me and I saw her walk over to Amy, who was sitting beneath a tree, lost in her own thoughts and sorrow for me. I couldn't hear them from such a distance, but I trust Faith continued the conversation; “Amy, can we chat?" Faith asked. "I believe I finally understand. I can see a new kind of love in his eyes, and I agree that we shouldn't let him suffer like this."

With tears glistening in her eyes, Faith returned to me, planting a gentle kiss on my head before settling down on the ground beside me. Shortly after Amy came back over, she and Faith continued their conversation.

It was the weekend, and despite feeling down, they were devoted to caring for me, ensuring I was well-fed, clean, and surrounded by love beyond my wildest dreams. I was relishing every moment with them. Faith had a profound impact on me; she truly saved me. A storm was approaching, so they needed to figure out how to get me into a stall. Having done it before, they quickly grabbed the tarp and truck to assist in moving me. JD chose to lie on the tarp with me, he was a cool guy, and

I liked him too. He was holding me to keep me calm. While Faith walked alongside and Amy drove the truck, Faith kept urging me to stay relaxed. I remained surprisingly calm, understanding that they were moving me for my own safety.

They nearly got me into the stall but realized it would take one more roll. You must remember I weigh about 800 to 1000 lbs. Luckily, Amy had a couple of friends stop by, and instead of rolling me, they all pulled on the tarp to get me inside. I expressed my gratitude; I attempted to stand but fell back into the hay.

Once I settled, they walked away, and I could hear them talking. Amy called the vet, knowing I couldn't continue like this. Then I saw Faith step away in tears and head back to me, she wanted to cherish every second with me, sitting in the stall, giving me treats, and chatting with me and I responded with soft sounds, you know we don't talk but we can make sounds, and we were having a conversation.

I watched Faith step out of the stall and walked over to the fence; she was overwhelmed with emotion. My own emotions were getting hard to handle as well. I watch as my buddy Tuff approached her as if sensing her need for comfort. He gently wrapped his head around her neck, pulling her close in a tender embrace.

Amy and JD looked over and they couldn't help but feel the warmth of the moment as it became clear that Tuff understood her feelings.

"Do the animals know, or is this God's way of telling me that it is His time for Remy?" Faith asked. The silent response was her answer.

Surprised yet grateful, Faith hugged Tuff back, realizing how special this connection was; it was a beautiful reminder that horses can truly feel and empathize.

Faith came back to my stall, and I realized that her hope for a miracle was fading. Yet, she found solace in the thought that perhaps in that picture it was God reassuring her that everything would be all right, that it was time for me to come home.

I found myself grappling with the reality of my condition, struggling to comprehend the fate that awaited me. While it was difficult to accept that I could no longer walk, I discovered a sense of calm I hadn't anticipated as the end approached. Instead of fear, I felt a profound understanding of our journey together and the challenges we faced, allowing me to embrace the inevitable with a sense of peace.

As Faith and JD departed from the farm, their journey was far from over. Faith took a moment to reflect on the events that unfolded next, revealing the twists and turns that awaited them beyond the familiar fields. Although the tears flowed freely, she returned home feeling heartbroken, aware that the upcoming moments would be more challenging than she could fathom. Her mind wrestled with the thought of not being able to witness his passing, but her heart urged her to be present.

He had loved and trusted her, and she needed to be there, believing that God would care for him, ensuring Remy received the comfort he deserved. Amidst her turmoil, this weighed heavily on her, but she understood that she needed to be strong for Remy, who relied on her support.

The restless night made the morning feel even more challenging for Faith and JD as they quietly made their way to the farm, both weighed down by sadness. Upon arrival, they found the farm bustling with activity; the farrier was busy with the other horses, and the vets were expected soon.

Faith quickly jumped out of the truck and headed to the stall, where she discovered me lying against the fence, having struggled to rise during the night and injuring my leg in the process.

She lovingly cared for me, offering me my favorite peanut hay and treats, speaking softly to reassure me of God's goodness and the promise of relief from pain, as well as a joyful reunion with my friends, Paint and Sugar. As tears streamed down Faith's face, she confided in me about the relentless search for a cure, feeling as though she had let me down despite their efforts. I, however, understood the depth of their struggle and didn't want to leave.

Remy looked at Faith, "*it's time for me to run free with Paint and Sugar.*"

"I won't forget, Remy. I will tell your story. If I can help one other horse…" Faith promised!

She shared with me the significance of the book, emphasizing that my legacy of raising awareness about some of the dark realities of the horse industry would one day save other horses. I guess, one day I will turn out to be the Star they always tried to make out of me. There are so many beautiful people, like Horse Haven Retirement Farm, and many others within the horse industry, and we all agree there is no room for abuse.

Embracing me tightly, she reminded me of the love we shared. Although Faith could never truly be ready to say goodbye to me, she realized that holding on out of selfishness was not the answer; it was time to face the reality of letting me go. I think she knew too that I was not wanting to leave her either. As Faith and JD spent precious hours with me, Amy joined us, providing me with familiar comfort. When the vets arrived, Faith felt an unexpected calmness wash over her, a gift from me for all the good she did for me. She no longer had to worry about me; I was confident I would be fine. My main concern was for her heart.

While holding me close, Amy prepared Faith for the procedure, explaining what to expect. Faith seemed so focused on maintaining my peace that it was unclear whether she was truly absorbing what anyone else was saying.

Faith invited JD and Amy to join her inside the stall, but they chose to remain by the fence. You can tell that Faith will always cherish me in ways that words cannot express, holding me forever in her heart. Throughout the process, Faith never broke eye contact with me, continuously whispering words of love and comfort until my soul peacefully flew away. As we gazed into each other's eyes, my unwavering gaze remained fixed on her, and as I departed, I prayed Faith felt the unique peace that only I could impart, as I embraced her one last time. *"Thank you, Faith!"*

Even after my spirit departed, Faith and JD lingered, honoring me with a small cross they hung in the stall, deciding to bury me with it and Faith's beloved sweater I used to rest my head on, while Amy braided the cross into my mane and JD collected a lock of my hair as a final tribute.

The tribute they left for me is something I will always carry with me. As I passed, I lingered for a moment and felt the sadness around me. I hope that the lock of hair they took serves as a reminder of the beautiful mane she once brushed routinely, symbolizing how profoundly you changed my life. You sent me to heaven without fear, filled instead with love and trust, the greatest act of mercy. I will miss you all dearly until we meet again. Although horses can't talk "*I Love you*."

faith

While Faith and JD were in the stall, they noticed Tuff standing nearby, observing them. As JD and Faith climbed over the stall fence, they watched Tuff approach the fence to connect with Remy.

This photo captures a moment before Remy passed away, with Tuff constantly looking after him. They like to believe that Remy's spirit also bid farewell to Tuff; saying, "*Until we meet again, my friend.*" And Tuff replied, *"We'll take it from here, buddy."*

As they made their way back to the barn, they continued to see Tuff paying his respects to his friend. With work ahead of Faith and JD, they had to leave, but Faith managed to gather herself and deliver her presentation, channeling her love for Remy into the moment, focusing on the cherished memories rather than the loss. That evening, JD and Faith visited the farm to honor Remy at his unmarked grave, located next to Sugar, who had passed away in Amy's arms a few years prior. Although JD and Faith never met Sugar, Amy spoke fondly of her, recalling how she was a sweetheart rescued alongside Remy and Roy.

Faith was deeply missing Remy, feeling a profound sense of loss, yet she recognized that the other horses also needed her affection. On her next workday at the farm, she found herself searching for Remy, overwhelmed by sadness.

Faith looked at Amy, “I can’t believe he is gone!”

“Honestly, Faith, I believe that the only reason you ever met Remy was to save him! You gave him love when no one else could. Now, you have to continue to share that love!”

Faith nodded, hoping that God would share a sign…looking for a reassurance that everything would be okay!

When Faith first met Remy, she felt a strong sense of purpose, because he was getting older, wanting to ensure he experienced love and trust before he ever left this earth.

She believed she had fulfilled that mission, as Remy left her with a heart full of love and trust, which brought her immense peace. While she felt she had helped him, Remy also provided her with comfort, his spirit easing her worries. Although the other horses offered similar support, her bond with Remy was unique, and he would always hold a special place in her heart. Faith knows the heart of a horse and now more than ever connects with them.

After a long day of work at the farm, Faith captured her usual photos and videos to promote awareness and gather donations for the farm. While driving with JD, she noticed a striking image on a stall, illuminated by the sun, which formed a beautiful cross.

When she tapped on it, the image enlarged dramatically on the tree's bark in front of the stall. Stunned, she paused for

a moment, unable to believe her eyes, and urged JD to stop the truck so he could see it too. JD was equally astonished, exclaiming it couldn't be real. Faith quickly called Amy, excitedly sharing the news and sending her a screenshot of the enlarged image. Upon receiving the text, Amy asked if it was what she thought it was, to which Faith confirmed it was indeed a picture of Remy's face on the tree. Curious, they rushed to the tree, only to find that the image had vanished, leaving them puzzled.

During that entire weekend, there were two other images that captured silhouettes of Remy. They can’t quite explain it, and perhaps they can't fully understand it, but whether Remy hasn't moved on yet and wanted to reassure them that he was okay remains a mystery.

Many of us have encountered butterflies, red cardinals, or other signs, but Faith had never seen an image of an animal or person who has passed away.

Faith remembered that she had asked for a sign. Perhaps the sign was only for her, or perhaps only for a moment. She now believed that everything was okay, for her, for Remy, and there was hope for the horses that came into her life. She was at peace with it all.

In her heart, Faith felt that Remy was genuinely concerned for her. As he licked her and nudged her goodbye, it was clear he sensed her heartbreak. Perhaps this was his way of reassuring her that he cared and wanted to ensure she was all right. We will never know but Faith knows Remy is now at peace.

Amy was away on a week-long trip, so Faith, JD, and Elizabeth decided to create a special memorial for Remy and Sugar. They ordered charming little tombstones and arranged bricks around the graves to surprise Amy, who had long wanted to honor Sugar. They decorated the area and added a bench for her to enjoy coffee in the serene countryside.

Eager to share the news, they FaceTime with Amy during her trip, and she was thrilled. Upon her return the next day, they all headed to the farm, where visiting Remy & Sugar became part of their daily routine.

As Faith and JD were leaving the gravesite, Faith mentioned leaving Remy his favorite treat, prompting laughter from JD, who reminded her to do the same for Sugar. Faith placed a treat on Sugar's grave as well.

Throughout the day, they worked alongside the other animals, but when Faith went to say goodbye to Remy, she noticed his treat was gone while Sugar's remained. She called Amy, Elizabeth, and JD over, and they all chuckled at the mystery of the missing treat. Amy suggested a squirrel might be the culprit, but they decided to embrace the idea that Remy was still with them in spirit, sharing a laugh over the situation.

A couple of days later, a dear friend of Faith, who loves horses and admires their dedication, wanted to visit the farm. She met the horses, but as it was getting dark, they decided to show her the gravesite they had built. Suddenly, she asked about some horses she thought she saw, and her friend pointed in the direction. Faith looked but concluded it was probably just some of the horses, so they hopped on the golf cart to investigate, only to find no horses around.

Faith asked what she had seen, and as she described one horse, it matched Remy perfectly, and continued to describe the other with very unique characteristics. Faith mentioned that they didn't have a horse fitting that description. Faith went home thinking nothing of it. Then she remembered Paint and after some thought, Faith texted the former owner of Remy and Paint, asking for a picture of Paint, Remy's best friend. When the picture arrived, Faith was astonished, realizing that the other horse she described was indeed Remy's best friend who had passed away several years ago and had never been on the farm. Faith reached out to her friend to talk about that other horse again, and after a brief conversation but no details at that moment of Paint's passing, Faith offered to send a picture. Her friend quickly recognized the horse, saying "Yes that is the other horse I saw" and asked where it was now. There was a moment of silence before Faith replied, revealing that the horse had passed away before Remy. The phone fell silent, and her friend could only respond with disbelief.

This farm, along with Amy, Faith, Elizabeth, and JD, held a special place in Remy's heart. It seems likely that he brought his best friend here to share a glimpse of their lives and the beauty of their surroundings. May these boys always run free.

I doubt any of them will fully grasp what they've experienced. The afterlife may be more enigmatic than they realize, and unclear why Remy appears to be sending them signs of his presence. Like you, they can only accept that this situation is beyond their imagination.

Ultimately, all they can do is have faith that while God may be a mystery to some, others may see Him differently.

They wished and prayed that Remy could have been with them for many more years, yet they understand that his story continues in a different way. Even though heaven has taken their beloved boy, Remy will forever remind them to show kindness and love to horses.

These magnificent creatures have emotions and remarkable hearts, and now they grasp the essence of a horse, knowing how he was cherished and graced by an angel. If there is a spiritual sanctuary, Horse Haven Retirement Farm is undoubtedly it, and the presence of

God is genuinely felt here. Even unanswered prayers can give hope for eternity.

Remy found a renewed sense of love and trust during his journey, creating a profound connection with Faith. By sharing Remy's story in this book, they aim to enlighten others about the genuine hearts of horses.

They take comfort in the knowledge that Remy left this world not out of choice, but because it was simply his time. Now, they hold dear the image of him galloping freely alongside Paint and Sugar. While they can only imagine, it feels as though he has checked in on them, offering reassurance of his tranquility, allowing them to bid farewell and share their love, just as he had always done. Particularly memorable was the day he departed in Faith's arms, surrounded by those who cherished him. As Amy noted, Remy was not one to show affection through licking, yet on the day he passed, he licked Faith, conveying a heartfelt message of love, gratitude, and goodbye. Run Free Remy you will always be missed and loved.

It seems that Remy might not be quite ready to let go just yet, or perhaps he's holding off until his book reaches its final chapter. Regardless of the reason, he has certainly crafted his own conclusion to his narrative. In doing so, he expresses a deep sense of love and trust, taking a moment to show his gratitude to those who have supported him along the way. This time, he's firmly in control of his story, steering it in a direction that feels right for him, and it's clear that he wants to share this journey with us.

We may never fully understand the reasons behind the signs Remy sent us after his passing, but one thing is clear: he had a purpose that resonated deeply, just as Faith had her own purpose in loving him. Remy's mission seemed to be to ensure that the love and connections we shared were not in vain. His presence, even in spirit, served as a reminder of the profound impact he had on our lives and the importance of cherishing those bonds. In this way, he continues to guide us, encouraging us to embrace our own purposes and to honor the love that remains, horse abuse awareness, taking the reins of meaning that transcends the boundaries of life and death.

To support Remy's memory and assist other

senior horses in need of rescue and a forever home, where they are not only fed, groomed, and loved but also, they heal their hearts and minds, please check out the Horse Haven Retirement Farm Facebook page.

In loving memory of our retirees Skippy, Sugar, and Remy

May you run free with love in your hearts for eternity.

REMY'S FRIENDS

JUST ENJOYING THE MOMENT

FRIENDS ARE THE BEST

SOMETIMES YOU JUST NEED TO TAKE TIME FOR YOURSELF IN THE COUNTRYSIDE

It always
protects,
always trusts,
always hopes,
always perseveres,
LOVE
NEVER
FAILS
1 corinthians 13:7-8

Moments we don't forget

FARM LIFE

Empathy of Horses

We love our friend Remy

Happy Guy

Holiday fun at the farm

More of Remy's Friends

Horses not only heal our own soul, but they also touch our hearts. Remy and Roy the colors of beauty, the eyes of love.

Nutrition for Horses

Potato Patch Inc.

Since 2007, we have been researching, formulating, using, re-formulating, and perfecting our herbal formulas for horses. This started due to a personal show horse of our's contracting EPM, and having used many semi-effective to ineffective treatments as per vet prescriptions in the past, we decided to go down the rabbit hole and find out as much about the disease – which isn't a disease at all but a parasite – as we could. That brought us to our Wormless recipe which rid the above-mentioned horse's EPM parasites and he went on to be a multiple World and Reserve World champion.

Due to the effectiveness of this formulation and our protocol, we started wondering what other ailments we could assist our horses with. Ulcers? You betcha. Trouble with mare's getting in foal? No problem. Poor semen quality? Not anymore. That evolved into developing our own daily vitamin mixture, joint and bone supplement, sleep deprivation assistance, adrenal support for those oddities and non-sweaters, and finally a complete supplement that is a combination of them all. It is our hope that our natural, earth-based nutritional and supportive supplements can help your equine's as they have helped our own.

Note: this is currently an incomplete list of everything we offer. Bear with us as we develop logos and get the site set up. If you have need of adrenal support, calming and sleeping assistance, a daily supplement for all your horse's nutritional needs, or a complete supplement to cover all of your bases, please email us at potatopatchfarms@gmail.com.

Potato Patch Inc.

We extend our heartfelt gratitude to Peggy for her unwavering support and assistance. We will always appreciate the extra time she provided us, even though Remy could not be cured. The additional time allowed us to cherish precious moments with him.

We can gain valuable insights from one another, and it's truly heartwarming to know that there are others who share the same passion for horses. When you find yourself in need of support, it's reassuring to have a community of fellow horse lovers ready to lend a hand.

Horse Haven Retirement Farm

WEBSITE: **https://www.horsehavenretirementfarm.com/FACEBOOK PAGE NAME**: Horse Haven Retirement Farm, Inc.

Their story starts with a question.......

What is something that you've always wanted to do, but haven't done yet?

The answer to that question for me is easy because it is something that I have wanted to do for as long as I can remember. I have always dreamed of opening a permanent retirement home for senior and elderly

horses where they could live the remainder of their lives stress-free in peace and security. A place where they would be provided with the proper healthcare, nutrition, lots of room to roam, lots of love and respect, and allowed to just simply be horses. A place where nothing is expected of them except to be happy.

In March of 2022, we took a leap of faith which was the first step in making this dream become reality. We purchased property which would become Horse Haven Retirement Farm. It has been a labor of love, determination, sweat, long days and sore backs, but that property has truly been transformed into a place where we can provide sanctuary for these deserving creatures. With the support of our family, friends, and our community, we are so proud to be making a difference for all of our "retirees"! They come to us from various backgrounds and with different stories; some happy, some sad, and some heartbreakingly tragic. Each one has worked their way into our hearts and become beloved family members to us!

So that's our story to date, and as we continue to write more chapters in this gratifying endeavor, we appreciate your prayers and thank you for your interest. If you would like to be a part of our mission, we do accept and appreciate donations, as we are a non-profit corporation, relying on the generosity of others who share our love and respect for these horses.

Thank you for visiting our website,

Sandra (Sam) and Scott Suber

What makes Horse Haven Retirement Farm special?

We provide a permanent retirement home for aging horses. Our commitment to these horses is that we don't sell or re-home the horses that come to live at Horse Haven. Once they're with us, they are home.

Disclaimer

Some names and identifying details have been changed to protect the privacy of individuals. Although the author and publisher have made every effort to ensure that the information in this book was correct at press time, the author and publisher do not assume and hereby disclaim any liability to any party for any loss, damage, or disruption caused by errors or omissions, whether such errors or omissions result from negligence, accident, or any other cause. This book is not intended as a substitute for the medical advice of veterinarians. The reader should regularly consult a veterinary in matters relating to health, particularly with respect to any symptoms that may require diagnosis or medical attention.

Please note that while this book may mention or feature a business and its offerings, the author is a client. This mention is for informational purposes only and does not constitute an endorsement or guarantee of specific outcomes. Readers should conduct their own due diligence and make decisions based on their individual needs.

Acknowledgements

I want to express my deepest appreciation to our readers for accompanying us on this journey. While this story may bring a sense of sorrow, it also underscores the profound impact of kindness and love in the healing of broken spirits of horses. Our experiences in the afterlife have left us in wonder, revealing mysteries that inspire hope in the existence of something greater than ourselves.

I am particularly grateful to Editor Ron Fraser for his invaluable guidance in reshaping Remy's story. My heartfelt thanks to Potato Patch Farm for their steadfast support and the wealth of knowledge they shared, as well as for allowing us to feature their page in this book. I extend my gratitude to the incredible friends and family who encouraged me throughout the writing process. Also, to my publicist, marketing expert Cynthia, for believing in our message and Remy's legacy.

I would like to extend a heartfelt thank you to Lynn for her invaluable support in strengthening our bond with

Horse Haven. Additionally, Norieta, Julie, Janet, Allison, Jerry, Stefania, Lori, Michelle, Faith, Alisa, Britney, Richard, Tyler, and Mira, who provided me with a comforting presence during Remy's journey, allowing me to share my emotions and find peace in their friendships. Also, thanks to some of these friends that provided feedback who reviewed the draft copy. With love to those that volunteer with us sometimes, Lynn, Faith, Anne, and Kathy who also watched Remy's heart and spirit change.

Lastly, I am profoundly thankful to Horse Haven Retirement Farm, which has provided me with the joy of volunteering and has become a beloved family, both human and animal. We absolutely adore the hearts of Sam, Donna and Scott, this sanctuary is a true blessing, ensuring the safety and happiness of its residents. Let us take a moment to raise awareness against abuse, for no being—human or animal—should endure suffering. Our hearts beat together, and our spirits can be delicate. Let us remain kind, stay safe, and, above all, continue to love and be loved.

Remy and Faith the bond for eternity

Standing in a field, face to face with a horse, offers a unique chance for self-discovery, mirroring our own purpose.. Just as we seek connection, horses are also in search of their person. If you are fortunate enough to encounter a remarkable horse or two, they will ensure you never feel alone. Faith shared a deep bond with many horses, but her connection with Remy was unparalleled. His passing at the age of 27 felt premature, leaving a lasting imprint on Faith's heart. Their relationship has not only defined her as his person but also ignited a passion within her to advocate for other horses in need. I believe we all strive to do what is right, and this book is a vital step toward raising awareness about the emotional lives and hearts of horses. May we all be blessed, both animals and humans alike, with safety, freedom, and the ability to love.

Always and Forever

11:11

Shari Young & Remy

Made in the USA
Columbia, SC
25 November 2025

73977541R00109